DRUGS AND GANGS

Gangs exist all over the world.

THE DRUG ABUSE PREVENTION LIBRARY

DRUGS AND GANGS

Margot Webb

THE ROSEN PUBLISHING GROUP, INC.

NEW YORK

Published in 1995 by The Rosen Publishing Group, Inc.
29 East 21st Street, New York, NY 10010

First Edition

Webb, Margot.
    Drugs and gangs / Margot Webb. — 1st ed.
      p. cm. — (The drug abuse prevention library)
    Includes bibliographical references and index.
    ISBN 0-8239-2059-3
    1. Gangs—United States—Juvenile literature.
    2. Drug abuse—United States—Juvenile literature.
    I. Title. II. Series.
    HV6439.U5W45 1995
    364.1'06'60973—dc20   95-21952
                                                  CIP
                                                AC

Manufactured in the United States of America

Contents

Introduction

*T*he following happened to me a few years ago.

I was a teacher and counselor in an elementary school. I had a 12-year-old girl in one of my groups who never talked, never raised her hand, and never answered a question. Her name was Silvia. I tried to coax her out of her shell, but nothing worked.

One day she surprised me by approaching me: "I'd like to speak to you."

We sat down outside, away from everyone else. I asked, "What is it, Silvia?"

She looked around nervously before answering.

"It's about my brother, Juan. Last Christmas he walked out of the house toward his

Confiding your fears to a trusted adult can be the first step toward finding a way to change your circumstances.

car where he had hidden some presents. I watched him go."

Silvia began to shake. I put my arms around her.

"All of a sudden, another car came by. I heard gunfire and Juan fell on the sidewalk. He was shot in the head. The street in front of our house was filled with blood." Silvia began to cry. She put her head in her hands.

"A drive-by shooting?" I asked softly.

She shook her head. "A new gang," she whispered. "My brother belonged to a different gang. Now I'm scared all the time."

Silvia and I went to my office. We began

8 | to discuss her family. Then I noticed a teenager's face pressed against one of the windows. "Oh, no," Silvia wailed. "That's my older brother, José. He belongs to the same gang as Juan. He'll kill us both if he finds out I told you."

"Don't worry," I said, but I was still afraid.

I went to the office door and let José in.

"You're Silvia's brother? Are you here to pick her up?" Trying to stay calm, I pretended not to know anything.

José shut the door behind him, pulled out a gun, and held it to my head.

"I told you he'd kill us!" Silvia yelled.

"You be quiet," José commanded. "What'd she tell you, huh, Teach? You better let me know." He pressed the gun harder against my head.

I knew I had to protect Silvia as well as myself. "Your sister is very shy," I said, "and I asked her if anything was bothering her."

"It's none of your business." José's voice was low, menacing.

"Well," I went on, "she told me some of the girls already had boyfriends and that she felt left out. She said the kids make fun of her because she's shy. I told her a twelve-year-old didn't need a boyfriend yet. We just started to talk about all this when you came in."

Gang violence occurs in small towns and large cities.

10 | *José suddenly put his gun down. He turned to his sister.*

"Silvia," he said, "you know what Pop tell you. No guys! You listen to your teacher, you hear me?"

Silvia looked away from him and whispered, "OK." I was elated that the lie had worked.

"I'm sorry," José now turned to me. "I thought you two were talking about something else. Something my gang wouldn't like. We deserve respect. But you're OK. You keep protecting my sister. I appreciate it."

As José left the office, he had one more thought.

"I know you've got a cool red car out in the parking lot. Me and my guys will see that nothing happens to it." He left.

I shuddered. Silvia slowly got up and asked, "May I come to see you again?"

I hugged her.

"Any time. My office door is always open." I winked at her. "We pulled it off, didn't we? Nobody was hurt."

Silvia's big brown eyes looked directly into mine. "Not this time," she said.

She ran outside. José and three other boys were waiting for her. They were all dressed in black, their gang color. They climbed into a brand-new black car to take Silvia home.

A few days later, Silvia came into my office. Her pale face told me something terrible had happened.

"I'm going to a funeral," she explained with a deep sigh. "My brother José was murdered two days ago. He was selling drugs for the gang, and we think a big dealer killed him."

Drugs are any substance that changes your body's chemistry. Alcohol is considered a drug.

CHAPTER 1

What Are Drugs?

*D*rugs are substances that change your body's chemistry. Some drugs are legal. They are considered medicine and are sold by prescription. Doctors prescribe these drugs to help a sick person get well or feel relief from pain.

There are also many illegal drugs, including legal medicines sold to people for whom they were not prescribed. Anybody can buy these drugs. In fact, you may already have been approached by a drug dealer in school or on the street. Maybe some of your friends do drugs. Perhaps you've tried one or two yourself. What you probably don't know is how much damage they can do to your mind, body, family, and life.

Some people take drugs to increase their energy or because they feel depressed.

Who Uses Drugs?

Illegal drugs are taken by children as young as seven or eight years old and adults as old as eighty.

There are many reasons why people take drugs. Teens who have low self-esteem are often attracted to drugs. They may think they are not good-looking enough, or smart enough, or rich enough. They may think that drugs can make them feel better. Once the drug wears off, however, they are left feeling sick or shaky, and they need more drugs.

Sometimes drug abusers are people who have suffered terrible life events. Victims of physical or sexual abuse sometimes feel that it's their "right" to snort cocaine, smoke pot, or mainline heroin. After all, they think, at least the drug isn't hurting them. But they are wrong.

Drug users have a long list of "reasons" for using drugs:

- I broke up with my boyfriend or girlfriend.
- My parents won't get off my case.
- Everybody does it.
- My gang makes me do it.
- I can stop whenever I want.
- I'm hooked now anyway, so I might as well go on.
- I just can't stop.

It is never too late to stop using drugs. Even if you are addicted and feel that you *can't* stop, there are people who can help. This involves asking for help, which is discussed in more detail later on.

Dangers of Specific Drugs
Amphetamines and barbiturates
Many teens take amphetamines or "speed." These drugs are man-made and

16 | come in the form of pills. They speed up the central nervous system, increasing the heart rate and raising blood pressure. In the beginning, the user feels as though he has unlimited energy, that he can do anything. But soon the user finds that he can't sleep and that he has no appetite. His heart may also be beating too fast. Finally his heart collapses.

Some amphetamines are prescribed by doctors for weight loss. Others are sold over the counter in pharmacies. Both types are addictive. Both types can be destructive if abused.

Barbiturates, or "downers," are sedatives. They slow down the functioning of all parts of the brain. Sometimes people who are addicted to amphetamines take barbiturates to slow down and get some sleep. Other times people take barbiturates to "mellow out" or relax. Barbiturates can also be prescribed by a doctor to calm the nerves. For people who have suffered a great trauma, such as the death of a loved one, a divorce, or the loss of a job, barbiturates can be helpful. They are beneficial only if they are taken by the person for whom they were prescribed, in the amounts indicated by the prescription, and for the length of time ordered

Members of your gang may try to encourage you to use drugs like marijuana to draw you further into the gang.

by the doctor. Like amphetamines, they are destructive if taken in any other way.

Marijuana. Marijuana, a drug made from dried leaves of the *Cannabis sativa*, or hemp, plant, was once considered a mild drug. During the 1960s and 1970s, students in high school and college smoked pot at parties and in their dorm rooms. They thought they were cool. It relaxed them, they claimed.

These people were mistaken. Pot is not a mild drug.

Scientists have since discovered that marijuana users have a shorter span of

18 attention, that they suffer long-term memory loss, and that their children may be born with birth defects.

Cocaine. Cocaine, derived from the coca plant, is a very dangerous drug because it is highly addictive. It is most often snorted through the nose. With repeated abuse, the tender tissue on the inside of the nose becomes raw and irritated. Eventually, the nose is so damaged that the user can no longer smell anything. Finally, the user can't breathe through his nose. Many coke users have nose surgery, but they usually go on using after they leave the hospital. All this agony is for a high that lasts only twenty minutes.

Another method of using cocaine is called freebasing. Cocaine is cooked over an open flame with alcohol to make it pure. It is then inhaled. Actor/comedian Richard Pryor scorched his face while attempting to freebase.

The worst danger from cocaine is similar to that of speed: It causes the heart to beat too fast. It can cause heart failure and death.

Heroin. Heroin, and its stronger form, China White, comes from the opium poppy. They are therefore called opiates.

Heroin is injected; China White can be smoked or inhaled. They are both very addictive, which means that a user needs more and more of the drug to achieve the desired effect.

Most people get sick and have severe headaches the first time they try heroin. These effects generally go away. Some users get diarrhea, muscle cramps, and stomach cramps. But by the time they discover this, they are addicted.

Because heroin is injected with a needle, another risk is acquiring the human immunodeficiency virus, or HIV, the virus believed to be the cause of AIDS, acquired immunodeficiency syndrome.

Alcohol. Many people don't realize that alcohol is a drug. This is probably because alcohol is legal for those over the age of 21. However, it is a drug. It is possible to become addicted to alcohol, like any other drug. Alcohol abuse has lifelong effects on the user's heart and liver and can kill the user if abused long enough or in large enough amounts. Baseball legend Mickey Mantle suffered such severe liver damage that even a liver transplant could not save his life.

Some teens mix drugs and alcohol. This is a deadly combination. The user

Gangs form for many reasons, one of which is to deal drugs.

risks brain damage, a coma, or even death.

Knowing what drugs can do to your body, your life, and your family and friends might make you think twice before taking drugs in the first place. It may also help you beat the temptation of selling drugs, especially if you belong to a gang.

CHAPTER 2

What Is a Gang?

It is estimated that there are nearly 55,000 youth gang members in the United States alone. Gangs in the United States range from small ones of only four members to huge groups that stretch across the entire nation. Their memberships run into the thousands. Large gangs usually have headquarters in cities like New York, Chicago, or Los Angeles, but they have branches in small towns across the country. Many of these gangs have become wealthy and powerful by dealing drugs.

Many people believe that gangs exist only in the big cities. They are mistaken. Their headquarters may be in New York or Los Angeles, but it is their business to

22 create smaller branches in many smaller cities.

- Atlanta, Georgia: John belonged to a gang. He was shot in the back and died at the hands of a rival gang.
- Chattanooga, Tennessee: José was arrested for killing a sixteen-year-old girl from another gang.
- Davenport, Iowa: Justin Voelkers, Anthony Hoeck, and Jason Means were convicted of shooting and killing seventeen-year old Michelle Jensen. They belonged to the Vice Lords, a gang that has been around Davenport for 30 years. It has chapters all over the Midwest.

There is no particular pattern to where gangs are found. They are all over the U.S. Most gang members wear special clothes or accessories or throw signs (use hand signs to identify themselves to each other and the outside world). They often use graffiti to warn other gangs of their power and to mark off their territory or turf. Gang members often have gang handles, names given to them by the gang, such as J. Dog or Loco.

Gang members may seem as if they

Gang members are often faced with a life of violence—
something they may not have bargained for when they
joined their gang.

have it made. They usually have money in
their pockets, a supportive and protective
group of "brothers" or "sisters," and an
exciting lifestyle. What you may not see,
however, is that violence is a way of life
for most gangs.

Many gangs are armed with weapons
such as guns and knives. Guns especially
are necessary for gangs involved in drug
dealing. They are used to protect the
gang, get revenge, and protect the business. In 1991 there were over 350 gang-
related killings in Los Angeles alone.
Most people involved in these killings are

People who join gangs are often seeking a supportive "family."

gang members, but more and more frequently innocent bystanders are the targets of the bullets.

Some gang members are friendly and polite. They may not appear to be violent. You may have a friend who belongs to a gang and not even know it. Perhaps such a friend offers you a joint or a couple of pills to boost your energy one day. If so, he may be a drug dealer. It is likely that he was sent by a large, well-known gang to sell in your neighborhood or school.

What you need to remember is that, large or small, gangs are dangerous. Once you buy drugs from them, or even consider selling drugs for them, you are no longer safe.

Who Joins Gangs?

Gangs consist of all kinds of people, regardless of age or race. There are specifically African-American, Asian, Latino, and white gangs. There are racially mixed gangs. There are also boys' gangs and girls' gangs.

People who join gangs are usually looking for something they don't get at home: love, attention, protection, friends, structure, money, or power. Gangs offer a sense of security and strength. They offer their members the ability to contribute something, a feeling of control over what's happening in their lives. Gang members build bonds with each other; they look out for each other.

Gangs also require the complete loyalty of their members. Once you join a gang, you must comply with whatever they ask. You are no longer an independent person. You are one of a group. You put your life on the line for every member of that group every day.

In the words of Hershey McFarland, a member of the Imperial Gangsters,

All-girl gangs are growing in number.

"What matters is, 'Is you down?' When we go out and mob somebody, you got to be out there with us, throwing blows, pulling the trigger." He was quoted in the *New York Times* in May 1994.

In April 1994, several casinos in Las Vegas were raided by Los Angeles gang members. One hotel, the Flamingo, was robbed by new members who were proving themselves to their gang. After the robbery, they had to turn over most of the money to the older, more experienced members. They received very little of what they had risked their lives to steal. They were caught.

Josh

Josh was 13 years old and felt as if everyone had forgotten him. His parents never seemed to be around, and even when they were, they paid no attention to him. They didn't even ask to see his last report card!

One day, the kid who sat next to him in math class, Mike, cracked a joke with him about the teacher. Josh laughed, and from then on they were friends. About a week later, Mike offered Josh one of the pills he was always carrying around. He said it would make Josh feel great and help him forget about his parents. Josh shrugged and took the pill. A few minutes later he did feel great. He felt he could do anything. Even better, Mike asked him to join his "club." What Josh later realized was that the club was a gang.

Josh began selling pills to his classmates to help out his new "club." He also started taking more. He used the money he made to buy clothes that matched what everyone else in the "club" wore. He felt appreciated and liked; finally he was receiving the attention he didn't get at home.

One night he and a bunch of guys were hanging out at Mike's when suddenly gun shots shattered the window in the living room. To Josh's horror, Mike grabbed a gun

Loneliness can drive some people to join a gang.

from a drawer in the coffee table and began
shooting wildly out of the window. Screams
of pain and shouts for an ambulance were
heard. Suddenly, Mike spun around crazily
and fell head first on the living room floor.
Josh ran to the window in time to see two
boys drag another into a waiting car and
drive off. Josh headed for the door, but one of
the guys stopped him. He said that Josh was
a member of the gang, and he had to stick it
out with the rest of them. Whatever hap-
pened, he would be a part of it.

All Josh had wanted was love and atten-
tion. What he got was a sentence in juvenile
detention.

As you can see, the activities that gangs are involved in—revenge, dealing drugs, and running a neighborhood or turf—are dangerous by nature. Violence goes hand-in-hand with being a member of a gang, beginning with initiation into it.

Initiation Rites

Gang initiations are difficult. First, you have to prove your loyalty to the gang, and that you are not weak or cowardly, by committing a crime. If you work in a restaurant, you may be asked to spill hot coffee on a customer or to spit in his food to prove that you want to join the gang.

30 Or you may be asked to commit a more serious crime such as robbing a store at knife- or gunpoint or physically hurting someone. In one case, gang members stopped a car filled with teens and told the new member that he had to gouge out an eye of one of the car's captives with a screwdriver. "It's either him or you," he was told. The boy blinded one of the teens.

These acts are proof of loyalty to the gang. They show that you are willing to do anything the gang asks you to do.

The actual initiation is usually done by many or all of the members of the gang. One initiate, Lewis, was told that his initiation included the possibility that he could be jumped at any time by any of the seventy members of the gang he wanted to join. One day he was followed by several gang members. He was kicked in the face and ribs. He received a broken nose and ribs. Then they helped him up.

He was repeatedly attacked over the next week by various members of the gang. He was beaten and choked. He still has the scars from when he was cut by a gang member with a razor blade.

Finally, Lewis was invited to the gang

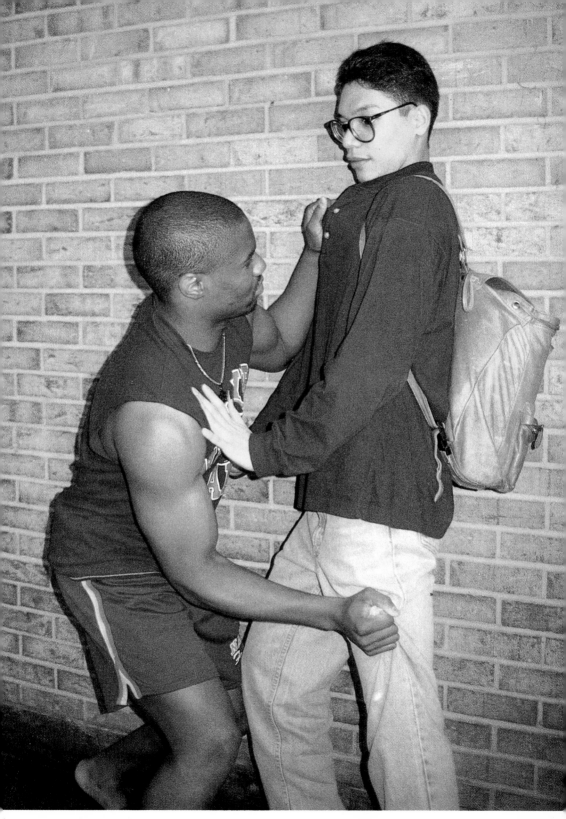

Initiation into a gang often involves some sort of beating.

leader's house. Once there, Lewis was given a knife and told to cut his own arm. He did, and the leader did the same. They then exchanged blood. Mark became a member of the gang.

In another instance, a woman pumped gas into her car, then went to the station's window to pay. As she turned back to her car, the station attendant motioned for her to return to him. She thought she'd given him the wrong amount of money, but that wasn't the problem.

"Listen, lady," the attendant said. "There's a guy hiding in the back seat of your car. I'll call 911. You go slowly to your car, open the door, and let's hope the cops are here by then."

She did as she was told. As she opened the door, she heard sirens. Quickly she closed the door and locked it from the outside. The police arrived and pulled a struggling 14-year-old boy from the back seat.

The boy refused to explain his actions at first, but soon he was scared enough to speak.

"It's my initiation into the gang," he mumbled. "My job was to kill someone." He pointed a finger at the woman. "I was gonna kill her."

Gang members face the same consequences as
everyone else for breaking the law.

34 "Do you know her?" another officer questioned.

"No. It didn't matter who I killed, just that I was tough enough to murder someone."

The teen was arrested and convicted. He is still serving time in a juvenile detention camp.

In yet another initiation ritual, gang members form two lines facing each other. The initiate runs through the line. The gang members can hurt him in any way they like. This is called "walking the line." If you live through it, you are in the gang.

Gang Life

Once in a gang, you may think your life has become exciting. You live on the edge of the law. You walk around the streets as if you own them. You may also peddle drugs to young kids, lining your pockets with their money and their futures. You may feel on top of the world. You should also know that your life is in constant danger.

Drive-by shootings began as acts of revenge on specific people, usually rival gang members. Today, anyone can be a target. Most gang members have bad

When you belong to a gang, especially a gang that deals drugs, you are putting your life on the line.

aim. You, as a gang member or not, could be walking alone or with friends or family and suddenly find yourself in the midst of gunfire.

Other drive-by shootings occur when gang members go to enemy turf and shoot into houses at random. Children who live in such houses are taught to crawl under tables if they hear gunfire. Thousands of children are killed in their own homes by drive-by shootings.

Turf wars are another fact of gang life. Gangs take certain streets or territories as their own. They make it impossible

36 for anyone to walk in "their" area without taking the chance of getting hurt. Each gang has its own turf. Wars take place about "owning" streets. If a member of one gang crosses the turf of the opposing gang, bullets fly. Members become soldiers fighting to the death. There is danger on every corner. In the end, all they have is their turf, a street that never really belonged to them in the first place.

Sometimes gang members get so excited in defending their territory, or taking revenge on those who have crossed it, that they end up shooting their own members. The police in one large city claim, "Gang members are terrible shots." The shooters are often too young to handle the powerful weapons to which they have access. They don't receive the proper training, nor do they usually have the strength to use the weapon properly. Thousands of innocent victims are claimed by these shooters every year.

Committing crimes other than selling drugs is a major occupation of many gangs. In one city, several young gang members decided to steal from a convenience store late one night. The owner saw five members come at him. He reached into his drawer, pulled out a gun,

and started shooting. He shot two kids
before he was killed. Upon hearing police
sirens, the three remaining gang members
ran out of the store and climbed a nearby
fence, hoping to get away before the police arrived. One kid had holes in his
sneakers. He found himself stuck on the
fence while bullets fired by his gang and
the police whizzed around his head. He
was struck by one and fell, dead. The
bullet belonged to one of his own gang
members. He was killed by someone who
was supposed to love and protect him.

Selling drugs, like throwing signs, is often part of gang culture.

CHAPTER 3

The Relationship Between Gangs and Drugs

Drugs are a billion-dollar business, and the heads of large gangs make most of that money. Gang members want to make money too, but they generally don't like to have a regular job. It's not cool. Often their answer is to sell drugs for the kingpins.

It is fairly easy to sell drugs. Many dealers begin by giving drugs to children or teens in school. "C'mon, just try it. You'll like it. Being high even makes math class fun." The person becomes addicted and begins to buy the drug. The addict generally doesn't have enough money to sustain his new drug habit, so he begins

Students are often prime targets for drug dealers.

to steal—from his parents, his friends, or even from strangers. He may even join the gang and begin to sell drugs to others to support his habit.

Life in a gang is a life of danger. You are in danger of death at every moment. The danger runs from the lowest position in a gang, that of a lookout, to the highest, that of the kingpin.

The Makeup of a Gang

The organization of a gang depends on how big or small it is. Small gangs have one leader and several followers. Older members are considered more important than younger or newer ones. Boys usually have higher status than girls. These smaller gangs are generally found in smaller towns and cities, or in suburbs of big cities. They are started by one person, who becomes the leader. They often disperse within a few years or are swallowed up by larger, better organized gangs.

Large gangs sometimes have thousands of members across the United States. Organized and efficient, they are run like businesses, which, in fact, they usually are. Their business is often to sell drugs.

There are several levels of gang membership.

Small gangs tend to have one leader and several followers.

- *Lookouts*—These gang members are usually between seven and ten years old. Their job is to watch the street while a drug deal or other crime is committed. If they see anything suspicious, such as the police or a rival gang member, lookouts give a warning signal to the gang members.

- *Initiates*—These are people who have proved their loyalty to the gang and are ready to go through whatever pain or torture the gang requires to become a full-fledged member.
- *Female gang members and girlfriends*— Many members of gangs are girls. There are also several all-girl gangs, equal in toughness and drug-running to the male-run gangs. These gangs are either independent or are considered sister gangs to certain male gangs. In general, gang members can go out only with members of their own gang. There is usually too much at stake to risk dating a member of another gang.
- *Neighborhood leaders*—Sometimes called *corporals*, leaders at this level may be in charge of 100 to 200 people. They have control over all their members, and all the money,

44

weapons, and drugs that flow in and out of the gang's possession.

- *Generals*—Also called *jéfes* or *honchos*, generals supply the neighborhood leaders with drugs, guns, and cars. These people report to the top level of power.
- *Kingpins*—At the very top of the gang is the kingpin, usually an adult. He has the ultimate power to decide what businesses the gang will enter, how to conduct business, and where. He has connections to drug suppliers in the United States and in the countries from which the drugs are bought. He makes the most money of anyone in the gang. He generally lives in luxury, while the rest of the gang members risk their lives to make money for him. Usually, the lowest members of the gang don't even know who the kingpin is.

The Myth About Selling Drugs

One of the biggest myths about being a member of a gang and selling drugs is that you'll get rich. Some people think that gang members are wealthy, that they drive around in expensive sports cars, and that they don't have to work to get all this

The life of a drug dealer is far less glamorous than many people think.

money. These people don't realize what goes on behind the scenes.

In reality, very few members get rich, even in gangs that deal drugs on a large scale. Although $300 a week sounds like a lot of money, working as a lookout or selling drugs is difficult and dangerous. You work every day, seven days a week— no weekends, holidays, or vacations off. You work from early in the morning until late at night. You are always on guard, looking over your shoulder for the police, rival gangs, or anyone who might infringe on your territory. You can't trust anyone

46 completely, not even your own gang members. And your life is always on the line. Every day you face the possibility of dying. All this to make $300 or $500 a week.

Some drug dealers do get rich, but even they are not safe from bullets or the police. Of the thousands of drug dealers that exist, only a few make enough money to call themselves rich. And even they are eventually busted or murdered.

Drug Use by Gang Members
People sometimes join gangs to support a drug habit started by that gang. They may begin to sell drugs or to prostitute themselves just to get their next fix.

Many drug dealers mix drugs with other substances, even gasoline, to make more money. They take out a little bit of the drug for themselves, and then add something to replace it. The additives are often poisonous. If you are an addict, chances are good you'll run into these mixed concoctions. You can become very sick or die from the poisons.

Daily Dangers of Gang Members
Gang members are constantly hunted by rival gangs. In addition, the police and

You may not even know where your gang gets
the drugs they sell.

PABLO EMILIO ESCOBAR GAVIRIA

SOLICITADO POR LA JUSTICIA

A QUIEN SUMINISTRE INFORMACION QUE PERMITA SU CAPTUR
EL GOBIERNO NACIONAL LE OFRECE COMO GRATIFICACION

$ 1.000'000.000.oo
MIL MILLONES DE PESOS

¡LLAME YA !

SANTAFE DE BOGOTA
2-22-50-12

GRATIS DESDE
CUALQUIER CIUDAD

¡ ESCRIBA

APARTADO AE

1500

This advertisement, delivered to newspapers in Bogotá, Colombia,
in August 1992, offered $1.4 million for information leading
to the capture of Pablo Escobar, drug lord of the Medellín
drug cartel.

the FBI have divisions that work specifically to break up gangs. They seize drug shipments, arrest gang members all the way up to the kingpin, and stop cartels, the groups selling drugs into the United States. All this begins with catching the dealer on the street.

New laws are being passed. One of the best known is nicknamed "Three Times and You're Out." This law states that if a person is convicted of committing a violent crime three times, he will receive a life sentence on the third conviction.

Help for drug abuse or involvement with a gang is only a phone call away.

CHAPTER 4

Staying Safe from Drugs and Gangs

You deserve to live a good life in a safe place, surrounded by people you love and trust. If you are not getting this from your family, try somewhere else. Look to other relatives or friends at school, or ask your guidance counselor, teacher, or clergyperson what you can do. Many people are available to help you.

If you are not in a gang, stay out. Don't join a gang out of boredom or the need to be tough. The toughest gang members don't expect to live a long life. If you are afraid you will be pulled into a gang, there are people who can help you. A list of numbers to call is given in the back of this book.

If you are already involved in a gang,

Friends or relatives who are not involved with drugs or
gangs can be a great source of support.

you still have a chance to get out. Some gangs will let you go if you agree to undergo a ritual much like initiation. This may involve a beating or other methods of inflicting pain. Even then, although the gang may say you are free, they keep a pretty close eye on you. You know things about the gang that they may not want others to know. Many cities have gang counselors who can help you figure out how to get free from your gang. That may involve moving out of the neighborhood, the area, or even out of state.

Avoiding Drugs

You already know what drugs can do to your mind and body. You know how being involved with gangs, either as a member or by buying drugs, can put your life in danger. Your life becomes controlled by drugs, dealers, and fear. Now you have solid reasons to avoid both drugs and gangs.

Maybe you are already a drug user, perhaps even an addict. The life of an addict is not pretty. It is horrible to be completely dependent on a substance. It reaches a point where nothing matters except getting the next fix. You may question why you should quit. The answer is

You might try talking to a peer counselor for advice on how to handle a difficult situation.

simple: What you are doing to yourself can kill you.

Drugs start out making you feel good. But after a while, you can't feel good unless you have taken the drug. You never feel normal. Without the drug, you feel weak and sick. You feel a terrible craving for the drug, so you take more. Soon you need so much of the drug just to feel alive that you are in danger of overdosing. Death is sitting on your shoulder when you are addicted to drugs.

In *Always Running: Gang Days in L.A.*, Luis Rodriguez tells about abusing uppers, downers, heroin, and alcohol while he belonged to a gang. The drugs and his lifestyle brought him to such a low point that he eventually wanted to commit suicide. He tried, but didn't succeed. Luckily, he received help and survived to write a book about his experiences to help other people see what the life of an addicted gang member is like.

Addicts can recover, but they can't do it on their own. There are several options, all of which involve asking for help. Don't give up hope.

It takes strength and courage to leave a gang, but your life is worth it.

Glossary
Explaining New Words

accessory   Article of clothing worn to complete an outfit.

addict   Habitual user of drugs or alcohol.

amphetamine   Chemical used to speed up the nervous system.

barbiturate   Chemical used to slow down the nervous system.

coma   Deep unconsciousness.

dependency   Need for someone to lean on and to make decisions for you.

depression   Feeling sad or worthless or out of control of your life.

gang   Group of youths banded together for social reasons.

gouge   Dig out.

initiation   Admission to a group.

kingpin   Main or essential person.

menace   To threaten.

narcotic   Drug used to relieve pain and induce sleep.

opium   Addictive narcotic drug prepared from the juice of the unripe seeds of the opium poppy.

For Further Reading

Baker, Donald. *Crips: The Story of the L.A. Street Gang from 1971–1985*. Los Angeles: Precocious Publishers, 1987.

Bing, Leon. *Do or Die*. New York: HarperCollins, 1991.

Booth, Martin. *The Triads: The Chinese Criminal Fraternity*. London: Grafton Books, 1990.

Campbell, Anne. *The Girls in the Gang*. Cambridge, MA: B. Blackwell, 1991.

Cervantes, Richard C., ed. *Substance Abuse and Gang Violence*. Newbury Park, CA: Sage Publications, 1992.

Currie, Elliott. *Dope and Trouble: Portraits of Delinquent Youth*. New York: Pantheon Books, 1992.

Daniel, Susie. *The Paint House: Words from an East End Gang*. New York: Harmondswork, Penguin, 1971.

Dawley, David. *A Nation of Lords: The Autobiography of the Vice Lords*. Garden City, NY: Anchor Press, 1973.

League of California Cities. *Drugs, Alcohol, and Gang Prevention Programs*.

Sacramento: The League, 1993.

Fong, Tim. "In Search of Recognition: A Former Teenage Gang Member Tells How He Changed His Life." *California Tomorrow*, vol. I, no. 2, Fall 1986.

Huff, C. Ronald, ed. *Gangs in America*. Newbury Park, CA: Sage Publications, 1990.

Harris, Mary G. *Cholas: Latino Girls and Gangs*. New York: AMS Press, 1988.

Hinton, S.E. *The Outsiders*. New York: Viking Press, 1967.

Mathews, Frederick. *Youth Gangs on Youth Gangs*. Ottawa, Canada: Solicitor General Canada, 1993.

Moore, Joan W. *Going Down to the Barrio: Homeboys and Homegirls in Change*. Philadelphia: Temple University Press, 1991.

Mowry, Jess. *Way Past Cool*. New York: Farrar, Straus & Giroux, 1992.

Rodriguez, Luis. *Always Running: Gang Days in L.A.* Willimantic, CT: Curbstone Press, 1993.

Shakur, Sanyika. *Monster: The Autobiography of an L.A. Gang Member*. New York: Atlantic Monthly Press, 1993.

Taylor, Carl S. *Girls, Gangs, Women, and Drugs*. East Lansing: Michigan State University Press, 1993.

Index

64 | About the Author

In addition to being an author, Margot Webb has been a teacher and counselor to children in the Los Angeles area of California.

Ms. Webb currently lives with her husband, an editor, in the Los Padres Mountain region, near Los Angeles, California.

Photo Credits

Cover p. 17 by Michael Brandt; p. 2 © Jim Tynan/Impact Visuals; pp. 7, 12, 42, 47, 52, 56 by Kim Sonsky/Matt Baumann; p. 20 © Donna DeCesare/Impact Visuals; p. 23 © Lisa Terry/Impact Visuals; pp. 24, 38 © Ted Soqui/Impact Visuals; pp. 28, 45 by Lauren Piperno; p. 31 by Katherine Hsu; p. 33 © Andrew Lichtenstein/Impact Visuals; p. 35 © Chris Takagi/Impact Visuals; p. 48 © AP/Wide World Photos; all other photos by Kathleen McClancy.